BEARCUB BIOS

NAOMI OSAKA

TENNIS STAR

by Rachel Rose

Consultant: Beth Gambro
Reading Specialist, Yorkville, Illinois

BEARPORT PUBLISHING

Minneapolis, Minnesota

Teaching Tips

BEFORE READING

- Look at the cover of the book. Discuss the picture and the title.
- Ask readers to brainstorm a list of what they already know about Naomi Osaka, including what they learned from the cover. What can they expect to see in this book?
- Go on a picture walk, looking through the pictures to discuss vocabulary and make predictions about the text.

DURING READING

- Read for purpose. Encourage readers to look for key pieces of information they can expect to see in biographies.
- Ask readers to look for the details of the book. What happened to Naomi Osaka at different times of her life?
- If readers encounter an unknown word, ask them to look at the sounds in the word. Then, ask them to look at the rest of the page. Are there any clues to help them understand?

AFTER READING

- Encourage readers to pick a buddy and reread the book together.
- Ask readers to name three things Naomi Osaka has done throughout her life. Go back and find the pages that tell about these things.
- Ask readers to write or draw something they learned about Naomi Osaka.

Credits:
Cover and title page ©Cal Sport Media/Alamy and ©LeArchitecto/iStock, 3, ©Kyodo News/Getty Images; 5, ©Paul Popper/Popperfoto/Getty Images; 7, ©Sean Pavone/Shutterstock; 8, ©/REUTERS/Newscom; 11, ©Mustafa Yalcin/Anadolu Agency/Getty Images; 13, ©VCG/VCG/Getty Images; 15, ©Kyodo News/Getty Images; 16, ©Matthew Stockman/Getty Images; 17, ©Al Bello/Getty Images; 19, ©Aflo Co., Ltd./Alamy; 21, ©bareMinerals/ MEGA/Newscom; 22, ©Kyodo/Getty Images; 23, ©Kyodo/Getty Images; 23, ©VCG/VCG/ Getty Images; 23, ©Kyodo News/Getty Images; 23, ©VCG/VCG/Getty Images

Library of Congress Cataloging-in-Publication Data

Names: Rose, Rachel, 1968- author.
Title: Naomi Osaka : tennis star / by Rachel Rose.
Description: Minneapolis, Minnesota : Bearport Publishing Company, [2022] |
Series: Bearcub bios | Includes bibliographical references and index.
Identifiers: LCCN 2020057408 (print) | LCCN 2020057409 (ebook) | ISBN 9781647478452 (library binding) | ISBN 9781647478537 (paperback) | ISBN 9781647478612 (ebook)
Subjects: LCSH: Osaka, Naomi, 1997---Juvenile literature. | Women tennis players--Japan--Biography--Juvenile literature. | Women tennis players--United States--Biography--Juvenile literature. | Haitian Americans--Biography--Juvenile literature.
Classification: LCC GV994.O73 R67 2022 (print) | LCC GV994.O73 (ebook) | DDC 796.342092 [B]--dc23
LC record available at https://lccn.loc.gov/2020057408
LC ebook record available at https://lccn.loc.gov/2020057409

For more information, write to Bearport Publishing, 5357 Penn Avenue South, Minneapolis, MN 55419. Printed in the United States of America.

Contents

Number One!

Pop!

Naomi Osaka hit the winning shot.

It made her the number one tennis player.

She was the best.

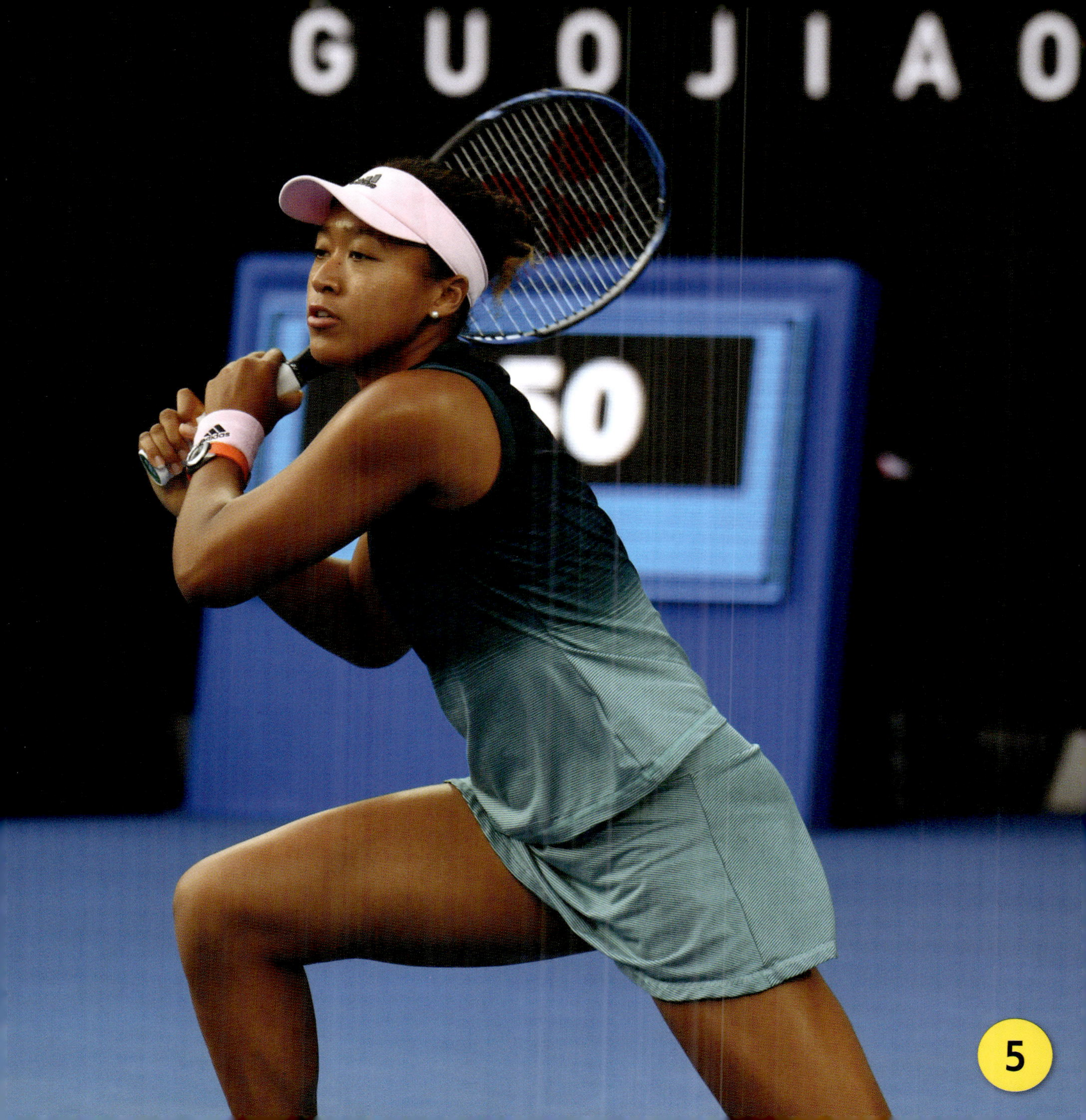
GUOJIAO

Naomi's Life

Naomi was born in Japan.

Her mother and sister were born there, too.

Her father is from Haiti.

Japan

Naomi's father

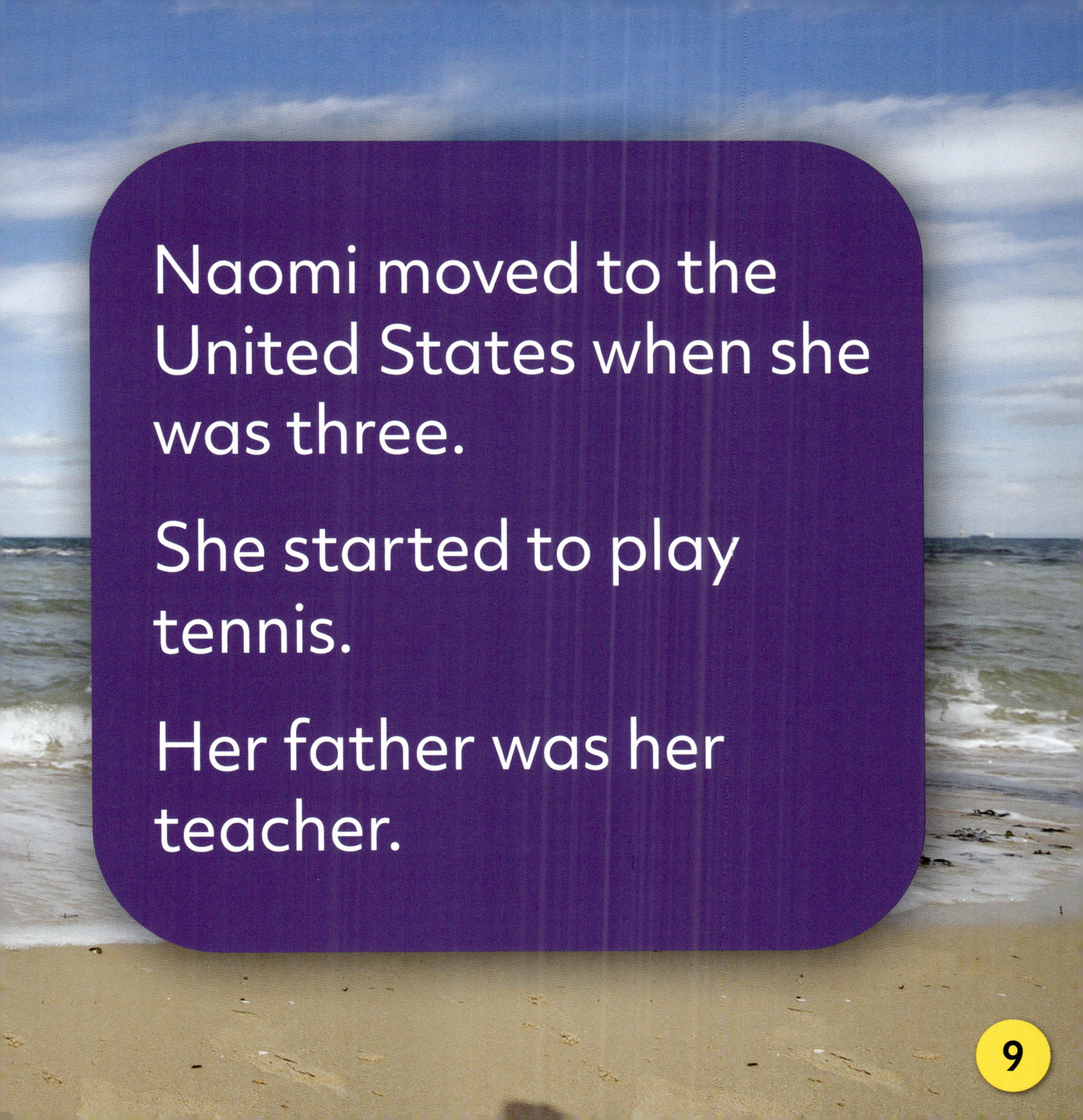

Naomi moved to the United States when she was three.

She started to play tennis.

Her father was her teacher.

Naomi worked hard.

She played well.

When she was 16, Naomi went **pro**.

Playing tennis was her job.

Naomi was very young to play pro.

But she won a lot.

She got a **prize** as the best new player.

Soon, Naomi played against people she had watched growing up.

And she won!

When she was 20, Naomi became the top women's player.

adidas
Australian Womens Singles Championship
NISSIN
adidas
adidas

What makes Naomi so good?

Her **serve** is very fast.

It goes faster than most cars!

NISSIN
ANA

Tennis changed Naomi's life.

She wants to help other girls play, too.

Naomi started sports groups for girls around the world.

The first one was in Japan.

Naomi is a star.

And she is young.

She still has so much time to play the game she loves.

Did You Know?

Born: October 16, 1997

Family: Tamaki (mother), Leonard (father), Mari (sister)

When she was a kid: She played tennis with her sister. Naomi lost to her sister more than 1,000 times!

Special fact: Naomi has a **manga** character based on her. Manga is a kind of Japanese comic book.

Naomi says: "I just really want to have fun with every match that I play because tennis is a game."

Life Connections

Naomi keeps playing tennis no matter what. Even when she loses, she keeps trying. Are there things that are hard sometimes? What do you do to keep trying?

Glossary

manga a kind of Japanese comic

prize something won for being the best

pro being paid to play a sport

serve a shot that begins play for each point in a tennis match

Index

Read More

Downs, Kieran. *Tennis (Blastoff! Readers: Let's Play Sports!).* Minneapolis: Bellwether Media, 2021.

Pincus, Meeg. *Naomi Osaka (My Itty-Bitty Bio).* Ann Arbor, MI: Cherry Lake Publishing, 2021.

Learn More Online

1. Go to **www.factsurfer.com**
2. Enter "**Naomi Osaka**" into the search box.
3. Click on the cover of this book to see a list of websites.

About the Author

Rachel Rose is a writer who lives in San Francisco. Her favorite books to write are those about people who lead inspiring lives.